THE TENNESSEE TITANS

BY

MARK STEWART

Content Consultant
Jason Aikens

NORWOOD HOUSE PRESS

CHICAGO, ILLINOIS

Norwood House Press
P.O. Box 316598
Chicago, Illinois 60631

For information regarding Norwood House Press, please visit our website at:
www.norwoodhousepress.com or call 866-565-2900.

PHOTO CREDITS:
All photos courtesy Getty Images except the following:
Topps, Inc. (6, 14, 17, 20, 21 both, 28, 34 right, 35 top left, 36, 40 both,
41 top and 43); Black Book Partners Archives (7, 9, 35 bottom left, 38,
and 41 bottom right); Matt Richman (48 top).
Cover photo: Ronald Martinez/Getty Images.
Special thanks to Topps, Inc.

Editor: Mike Kennedy
Designer: Ron Jaffe
Project Management: Black Book Partners, LLC.
Research: Evan Frankel

LIBRARY OF CONGRESS CATALOGING-IN-PUBLICATION DATA

Stewart, Mark, 1960-
    The Tennessee Titans / Mark Stewart ; content consultant Jason Aikens.
        p. cm.
    Includes bibliographical references and index.
    Summary: "Presents the history, accomplishments and key personalities of
the Tennessee Titans football team. Includes timelines, quotes, maps,
glossary and websites"--Provided by publisher.
    ISBN-13: 978-1-59953-203-5 (library edition : alk. paper)
    ISBN-10: 1-59953-203-4 (library edition : alk. paper) 1. Tennessee
Titans (Football team)--History--Juvenile literature. I. Aikens, Jason. II.
Title.
    GV956.T45S74 2008
    796.332'640976819--dc22

                                                    2008010531

Manufactured in the United States of America.

COVER PHOTO: The Titans celebrate a game-winning field goal during
the 2006 season.

Table of Contents

SPORTS WORDS & VOCABULARY WORDS: In this book, you will find many words that are new to you. You may also see familiar words used in new ways. The glossary on page 46 gives the meanings of football words, as well as "everyday" words that have special football meanings. These words appear in **bold type** throughout the book. The glossary on page 47 gives the meanings of vocabulary words that are not related to football. They appear in ***bold italic type*** throughout the book.

Meet the Titans

Football is a game of speed and power. The faster you move, and the harder you **block** and tackle, the better your chances of winning. The Tennessee Titans know all about these rules. They live by them.

The Titans play hard from the opening kickoff to the final gun. They never let up. Their hard-charging style has led to a lot of amazing victories over the years.

For Tennessee fans, fantastic finishes are a way of life. The Titans have a knack for winning close games, especially in front of their home crowd. This has been true since their first year—back when they played in another city and went by a different name.

This book tells the story of the Titans. They are a proud team with a *tradition* of working hard to stay a step ahead of their opponents. From their players to their coaches, the Titans have always done things their own way. Their fans have come to expect something surprising and different whenever Tennessee takes the field.

Keith Bulluck and Cortland Finnegan leap high in the air to celebrate a good defensive play during a 2007 game.

Way Back When

GEORGE BLANDA quarterback

The story of the Tennessee Titans begins in Houston, Texas. In 1960, a new **professional** football league known as the **American Football League (AFL)** was launched. One of the people who helped form the AFL was Bud Adams. He owned the team that would play in Houston. Adams called his club the Oilers, and they made headlines right away by signing college star Billy Cannon to a $110,000 contract. It was more than twice the amount that the Los Angeles Rams of the **National Football League (NFL)** had offered Cannon.

The Oilers chose George Blanda to be their first quarterback and kicker. He had been a member of the Chicago Bears in the NFL for many years. Blanda became a star in Houston and led the Oilers to the **AFL Championship** game three times. They won in 1960 and 1961, and lost a thrilling **double-overtime** battle in 1962. They also reached the AFL Championship game in 1967.

LEFT: George Blanda, the team's first great quarterback.
RIGHT: Warren Moon followed in Blanda's footsteps many years later.

The Oilers were an exciting, high-scoring club in their early years. In 1961, they became the first pro football team to score 500 points in a season. Houston often beat opponents with its great passing game. Blanda's favorite receivers were Bill Groman, Charley Hennigan, and Charley Tolar.

The Oilers had some good teams in the 1970s and 1980s. By then, they were part of the NFL's **American Football Conference (AFC)**. (The AFL had *merged* with the NFL in 1970.) Houston's offensive stars included quarterbacks Dan Pastorini and Warren Moon, receivers Ernest Givins, Haywood Jeffires, and Drew Hill, and kicker Toni Fritsch. Elvin Bethea, Ken Houston, Curley Culp, and Robert Brazile led the team's defense.

Houston's best player was Earl Campbell. He was a powerful runner who battered opponents. Campbell topped the NFL in rushing each season from 1978 to 1980.

From 1991 to 1993, the Oilers were one of the best teams in the NFL. Houston fans believed their club could reach the **Super Bowl**, but disaster struck in the **playoffs** all three years. Adams decided it was time to rebuild the team and moved it to Tennessee. In 1997, the Oilers left for Memphis. Over the next few years, the team opened a new stadium in Nashville and changed its name to the Titans.

The Titans relied on three rugged offensive stars—quarterback Steve McNair, running back Eddie George, and tight end Frank Wycheck. The defense was even tougher. It starred Jevon Kearse, Samari Rolle, and Blaine Bishop. In 1999, the Titans reached their first Super Bowl.

Age and injuries caught up with Tennessee in 2004. Once again, it was time to rebuild. The Titans **drafted** and traded for hungry, talented players to create a new foundation. Their goal was to find special stars like Blanda, Campbell, and McNair to lead them into the future.

LEFT: Defenders for the Kansas City Chiefs can't keep up with Earl Campbell.
ABOVE: Steve McNair, the quarterback who led the Titans to their first Super Bowl.

The Team Today

In 2005, the Titans were the youngest team in the NFL. Their fans saw that Tennessee had great *potential* and were willing to wait a few seasons for the players to grow up together. To their delight, the team made it back to the playoffs in 2007. The Titans won a lot of close games. Their fans knew that was the mark of a team on the rise.

The Titans were able to rebuild thanks to a good mix of *experienced* players and young stars. **Veterans** such as Keith Bulluck, Kyle Vanden Bosch, and Albert Haynesworth understood what it took to win in the NFL. They passed on that knowledge to players such as Michael Griffin and LenDale White.

One player who already knew how to win was Vince Young. He took over as Tennessee's quarterback in 2006. Young showed the leadership and desire to be a true superstar. Although Young and the Titans still have much to learn, their future looks as bright as any team in the NFL.

LenDale White and Vince Young joke around before a game during the 2007 season.

Home Turf

The Houston Oilers did not have their own stadium until 1968. They played in college stadiums from 1960 to 1967, and then moved into the famous Astrodome. The Oilers became the first pro football team to make its home in a domed stadium.

When the team moved to Tennessee in 1997, it spent one year in the Liberty Bowl in Memphis. In 1998, the team moved to Nashville and played in Vanderbilt Stadium until construction of a new stadium was completed.

The Titans' new stadium opened in 1999. It is located on the banks of the Cumberland River in downtown Nashville. It has had a couple of different names over the years, but most fans call it the Coliseum. The Titans have sold out every game since they moved there.

BY THE NUMBERS

- *There are 68,809 seats for football in the Titans' stadium.*
- *On April 16, 1998, the stadium was hit by a tornado while it was being built. It still opened on time.*
- *The Titans beat the Cincinnati Bengals 36–34 in the stadium's first NFL game.*
- *The Titans won the first 13 games they played in their stadium.*

Fans fill the Titans' stadium for a game during the 2005 season.

Dressed for Success

The Titans are one of the few teams in the NFL that has changed its name. Even so, the team's main color—light blue—has been the same since 1960. During their years in Houston as the Oilers, they also used red and white. Tennessee still features those colors, along with dark blue. The team has worn three different helmet colors over the years—blue, silver, and white.

When the team played in Houston, it paid tribute to Texas's oil industry. Houston's helmet *logo* was an oil derrick—a piece of equipment used for drilling. The Oilers also used a picture of an oil-field worker, or "oiler."

The name "Titans" was chosen after the team moved to Nashville. A titan is a giant described in ancient Greek myths. It is a good, strong-sounding name that was used in the early 1960s by the New York team that is now called the Jets.

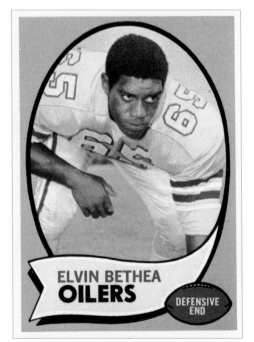

ELVIN BETHEA
OILERS

DEFENSIVE END

Elvin Bethea models the team's uniform from the 1960s.

UNIFORM BASICS

The football uniform has three important parts—
- Helmet
- Jersey
- Pants

Helmets used to be made out of leather, and they did not have facemasks—ouch! Today, helmets are made of super-strong plastic. The uniform top, or jersey, is made of thick fabric. It fits snugly around a player so that tacklers cannot grab it and pull him down. The pants come down just over the knees.

There is a lot more to a football uniform than what you see on the outside. Air can be pumped inside the helmet to give it a snug, padded fit. The jersey covers shoulder pads, and sometimes a rib protector called a flak jacket. The pants include pads that protect the hips, thighs, *tailbone*, and knees.

Football teams have two sets of uniforms—one dark and one light. This makes it easier to tell two teams apart on the field. Almost all teams wear their dark uniforms at home and their light ones on the road.

Albert Haynesworth wears Tennessee's dark blue uniform during a 2007 game.

We Won!

Back when the Tennessee Titans were known as the Houston Oilers, they were the top team in the American Football League. The Oilers were champions of the league's **Eastern Division** four times from 1960 to 1967—and the AFL champions in 1960 and 1961. Both times, the Oilers faced the Chargers for the title.

George Blanda was the star of the 1960 AFL Championship. After the Chargers went ahead 6–0, Blanda threw a touchdown pass and kicked a field goal to give the Oilers a 10–9 lead at halftime. Both teams scored in the third quarter to make the score 17–16. Early in the fourth quarter, Blanda had the Oilers on the move again. He threw a short pass to Billy Cannon, who broke a tackle and then outran the rest of the defense for an 88-yard touchdown. The Chargers **mounted** two drives into Houston territory, but the Oilers stopped them on fourth down twice—the last time with less than a minute to play. The Oilers won 24–16.

One year later, the same teams met again. The first game had been played in Houston. This time, the Oilers traveled to San Diego. The Chargers had moved there after spending the 1960 season in Los Angeles. San Diego fans watched a wild contest. There were seven **fumbles** and 10 **interceptions** in all.

The Oilers held a slim 3–0 lead in the third quarter when Blanda was forced to scramble. He looked downfield and threw a pass to Cannon,

who leaped high to make a great catch. When Cannon came down, he dodged one tackler and sprinted into the end zone for a spectacular 35-yard touchdown. The Chargers cut the lead to 10–3 in the fourth quarter. With two minutes left, San Diego was driving for the tying touchdown. Houston's Julian Spence stopped the Chargers with an interception. Once again, the Oilers held on for the AFL Championship.

The Oilers played in another thrilling championship game in 1962. In that contest, they faced the Dallas Texans (who would

LEFT: George Blanda drops back to pass.
ABOVE: Billy Cannon, a star for the champs in 1960 and 1961.

become the Kansas City Chiefs). Blanda led a furious fourth-quarter *comeback* to tie the score 17–17. Unfortunately, the Oilers could not pull out the victory. The Texans kicked a field goal to win in double-overtime.

Nearly four *decades* later, the Titans were part of another spectacular championship game. With Steve McNair and Eddie George leading the way in 1999, Tennessee made the playoffs and won the **AFC Championship**. The Titans played the St. Louis Rams in Super Bowl XXXIV. After trailing 16–0, Tennessee staged a great comeback. With three minutes left, the Titans tied the score at 16–16.

The Rams responded quickly with a long touchdown to take a 23–16 lead. McNair and the Titans did not give up. They moved down the field with the clock ticking away. On the game's last play, McNair passed to Kevin Dyson, who stretched for the goal line. Incredibly, he was tackled just a few feet short as time ran out. To this day, it is one of the Super Bowl's most fantastic finishes.

LEFT: Eddie George crashes over the goal line against the St. Louis Rams.
ABOVE: Kevin Dyson comes up just short of the tying touchdown in Super Bowl XXXIV.

Go-To Guys

To be a true star in the NFL, you need more than fast feet and a big body. You have to be a "go-to guy"—someone the coach wants on the field at the end of a big game. Fans of the Oilers and Titans have had a lot to cheer about over the years, including these great stars …

THE PIONEERS

CHARLEY HENNIGAN   Receiver

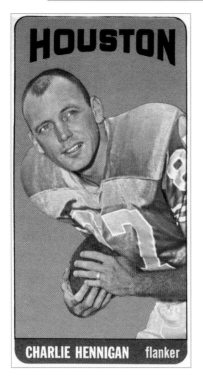

CHARLIE HENNIGAN flanker

• BORN: 3/19/1935 • PLAYED FOR TEAM: 1960 TO 1966

Charley Hennigan was a speedy receiver who had great *stamina*. Late in games, he was almost impossible to cover. Hennigan was the first player to catch 100 passes in a season. In 1961, he had 1,746 receiving yards—a record that stood for 34 years.

GEORGE BLANDA   Quarterback/Kicker

• BORN: 9/17/1927 • PLAYED FOR TEAM: 1960 TO 1966

Many pass defenders in the early days of the AFL were inexperienced. George Blanda had the arm and knowledge to take advantage of them. In 1961, he threw 36 touchdown passes in 14 games.

KEN HOUSTON
Defensive Back

- Born: 11/12/1944
- Played for Team: 1967 to 1972

Ken Houston was the best safety of his *era*. He was big and fast, and tackled opponents very hard. During his career, Houston intercepted 49 passes and returned nine of them for touchdowns.

ELVIN BETHEA
Defensive Lineman

- Born: 3/1/1946
- Played for Team: 1968 to 1983

Elvin Bethea was a cat-quick defensive end who loved to smash his way past blockers and **sack** the quarterback. In the 1970s, he and **nose tackle** Curley Culp gave the Oilers one of the best defensive lines in football history.

DAN PASTORINI
Quarterback

- Born: 5/26/1949
- Played for Team: 1971 to 1979

No quarterback was tougher than Dan Pastorini. He stood his ground even when a defensive player was inches away from him. Pastorini made the **Pro Bowl** in 1975.

LEFT: Charley Hennigan
TOP RIGHT: Ken Houston
BOTTOM RIGHT: Dan Pastorini

MODERN STARS

EARL CAMPBELL   Running Back

- BORN: 3/29/1955   • PLAYED FOR TEAM: 1978 TO 1984

Before his knees began aching, Earl Campbell was the NFL's most lethal weapon. He stood less than six feet tall but weighed more than 230 pounds. When Campbell started moving, there was almost no way of stopping him. He was named **All-Pro** in each of his first four seasons.

WARREN MOON   Quarterback

- BORN: 11/18/1956   • PLAYED FOR TEAM: 1984 TO 1993

Warren Moon won five championships in the **Canadian Football League** before joining the Oilers. No quarterback was better at throwing while on

the run. Moon led the NFL in passing yards in 1990 and 1991, and was the AFC's top-rated quarterback in 1992.

HAYWOOD JEFFIRES   Receiver

- BORN: 12/12/1964
- PLAYED FOR TEAM: 1987 TO 1995

For many years, Haywood Jeffires was Warren Moon's favorite target. Jeffires led the AFC in catches each year from 1990 to 1992. His best season was 1991, when he finished with 100 receptions.

LEFT: Warren Moon and Haywood Jeffires
TOP RIGHT: Steve McNair
BOTTOM RIGHT: Vince Young

STEVE MCNAIR   Quarterback

• BORN: 2/14/1973   • PLAYED FOR TEAM: 1995 TO 2005

Steve McNair was such a great runner that many doubted he could be a good passer in the NFL. He proved them wrong by leading the Titans to the Super Bowl in his third year as the team's starter. In 2003, McNair tied for first in voting for the NFL's **Most Valuable Player (MVP)** award.

EDDIE GEORGE   Running Back

• BORN: 9/24/1973   • PLAYED FOR TEAM: 1996 TO 2003

Eddie George never missed a game in eight years with the Titans and gained more than 1,000 yards in every season but one. George was named All-Pro for the third time in 2000 when he rushed for 1,509 yards and scored 16 touchdowns.

VINCE YOUNG   Quarterback

• BORN: 5/18/1983   • FIRST SEASON WITH TEAM: 2006

Vince Young played his way into the starting lineup in his first year. He led the Titans to six wins in a row and was named the NFL's Offensive **Rookie of the Year**. Young made a name for himself with his ability to lead his team from behind.

23

On the Sidelines

Few teams have had as many top coaches as the Oilers and Titans. Houston's first coach, Lou Rymkus, led the team to the 1960 AFL Championship. When Rymkus decided to retire from coaching, Wally Lemm took over. He guided the Oilers to the 1961 AFL Championship.

In the years after Lemm, the Oilers welcomed many other great coaches, including Sammy Baugh, Sid Gillman, Bum Phillips, Jerry Glanville, and Jack Pardee. Phillips and Glanville were two of the most *colorful characters* in the NFL. They were excellent leaders and well liked by players, fans, and sportswriters because of their sense of humor. Phillips, Glanville, and Pardee each brought the team to the playoffs four years in a row.

In 1994, Jeff Fisher was *promoted* from defensive coordinator to head coach. He taught his players to wear down opponents. No team worked harder at blocking and tackling—or made more big plays at the end of close games. Fisher led the Titans to their first Super Bowl.

Jeff Fisher talks things over with Vince Young during a 2007 game.

One Great Day

Vince Young had not been in the NFL for very long when the Titans met the New York Giants late in the 2006 season. Maybe that was a good thing. No one had told Young that winning a game when your team is losing 21–0 in the fourth quarter is nearly impossible.

The comeback began with less than 14 minutes left on the clock. After Tennessee intercepted a pass, Young went to work. Using his arm, legs, and head, he moved the Titans to the 4 yard line, and then threw a pass to Bo Scaife for a touchdown. The score was now 21–7.

The Titans played good defense and forced the Giants to punt. Tennessee returned the kick to New York's 36 yard line. Six plays later, Young scored on a one-yard run. The score was now 21–14 with less than six minutes left.

After more strong defense, the Titans got the ball back on their own 24 yard line. Young made two great runs and completed three passes. He finished off the **drive** with a touchdown toss to Brandon Jones. The score was now tied 21–21.

The Giants tried to win the game with 44 seconds left, but their strategy backfired. The Titans intercepted another pass. With time for just a few plays, Young completed two passes to get the Titans close enough for a field goal. Rob Bironas kicked it through the uprights for a 24–21 victory. Young had led the greatest fourth-quarter comeback in team history— and showed Tennessee fans that he was a truly special player.

Legend Has It

Who played the greatest game in the history of Monday Night Football?

Most Yards, Rushing, Rookie

LEGEND HAS IT that Earl Campbell did. The Oilers and Miami Dolphins played in front of millions of football fans on a Monday night in November 1978. For most viewers, it was their first chance to see Campbell. He was having a good rookie year, but no one was ready for what he did against one of the best defenses in the AFC. On his first 27 carries, Campbell barreled through the Dolphins for 118 yards and three touchdowns. On his 28th carry, he exploded past everyone for an amazing 81-yard touchdown to give Houston a 35–30 victory.

ABOVE: A trading card highlighting Earl Campbell's great rookie season.
RIGHT: Billy "White Shoes" Johnson

Did the Oilers help lead to the use of Instant Replay in the NFL?

LEGEND HAS IT that they did. In the 1978 AFC Championship game, the Oilers faced the Pittsburgh Steelers. Houston trailed 17–10 when Dan Pastorini threw a perfect pass to Mike Renfro in the back of the end zone. Officials did not think that Renfro had both feet in-bounds when he caught the ball, and they ruled the pass incomplete. The Oilers lost the game—and their chance to go to the Super Bowl. A television replay seemed to show that Renfro's catch was good. The following season, the NFL decided to let officials look at replays to help them make difficult calls.

Which player was named after his shoes?

LEGEND HAS IT that Billy Johnson was. Johnson returned kicks and punts for the Oilers in the 1970s. In seven seasons in Houston, he scored seven touchdowns on returns. Fans loved his *funky* end zone dances and the bright white shoes he wore on game days. Johnson was known far and wide as "White Shoes."

Team Spirit

Football fans in Tennessee have been rooting for the Titans since 1997. They have continued one of the NFL's great traditions. When the Oilers played in Houston, the fans there loved the team with all their heart. During the late 1970s, they often shouted, "Luv Ya Blue!" They wore Oiler-blue clothes and painted themselves Oiler-blue for games. They drove around Houston with Luv Ya Blue! bumper stickers and brought big Luv Ya Blue! signs to the Astrodome.

After the Oilers lost the 1978 AFC Championship in Pittsburgh, the players were very sad. When they stepped off the airplane in Houston, they were amazed to find 50,000 fans there to greet them. It was a Luv Ya Blue! party that the players never expected—and never forgot.

In their years in Tennessee, the Titans have also created a special bond with their fans. That includes Tennessee's team colors. The Titans—and their fans—continue to proudly wear the color blue.

LEFT: Keith Bulluck greets fans during the 2006 season.
ABOVE: An Oiler-blue pin from the team's days in Houston.

Timeline

In this timeline, each Super Bowl is listed under the year it was played. Remember that the Super Bowl is held early in the year and is actually part of the previous season. For example, Super Bowl XLII was played on February 3rd, 2008, but it was the championship of the 2007 NFL season.

1964
Charley Hennigan becomes the first player to catch 100 passes in a season.

1980
Earl Campbell leads the NFL with 1,934 rushing yards.

1960
The Houston Oilers are AFC champions in their first season.

1971
Ken Houston returns four interceptions for touchdowns.

1989
Bruce Matthews and Mike Munchak are both voted All-Pro.

A pin from the team's early days.

Ken Houston

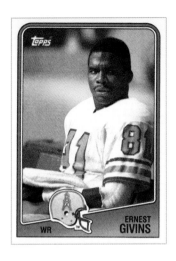

Ernest Givins

Steve McNair scrambles during Super Bowl XXXIV.

1992
Ernest Givins leads the AFC with 10 touchdown catches.

2000
The Titans play in their first Super Bowl.

2003
Steve McNair and Peyton Manning share the NFL MVP Award.

1990
Warren Moon leads the NFL with 33 touchdown passes.

1997
The Oilers move to Tennessee.

2007
Kyle Vanden Bosch makes his second Pro Bowl.

Warren Moon

Kyle Vanden Bosch

Fun Facts

WEIRD SCIENCE

One of the players the Oilers invited to their first training camp was a biology teacher who wrote the team asking for a tryout. His name was Charley Hennigan. He not only made the team, he finished his career with 410 catches and 51 touchdowns.

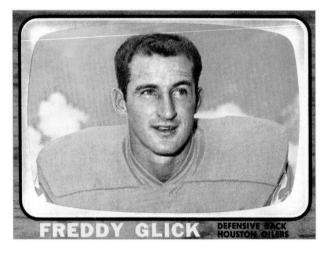

FREDDY GLICK DEFENSIVE BACK HOUSTON OILERS

MEN OF STEAL

The Oilers were known as a great passing team in the 1960s. They were also great pass defenders. Freddy Glick and Jim Norton combined for 75 interceptions from 1960 to 1968.

LARGE AND IN CHARGE

Jevon Kearse was so fast and so big that teammates nicknamed him the "Freak." When he spread his hand, his thumb and pinkie were more than a foot apart.

FORCE OF ONE

No defensive player in team history had a better day than Vernon Perry in the 1979 playoffs against the San Diego Chargers. He intercepted four passes and blocked a field goal in a 17–14 victory.

CANNON BALL

One of the best players in team history was Billy Cannon. He was a great runner and receiver. In a 1961 game, Cannon ran for 216 yards and caught passes for 114 more.

FAMOUS FRIENDS

Mike Munchak and Bruce Matthews were great linemen for the Oilers and Titans—and also very close friends. Munchak was voted into the **Hall of Fame** in 2001. His buddy Matthews joined him there six years later.

LEFT: Freddy Glick
RIGHT: Mike Munchak and Bruce Matthews at the Hall of Fame.

Talking Football

"I love this game so much it's ridiculous."

—Vince Young, on his passion for football

"I'm a selfish football player. Each time the ball is snapped, I tell myself that I want to make that tackle, make that big play."

—Jevon Kearse, on giving his best all the time

"I don't just play to be decent, average. I want to be the best I can be, and I don't know how good that is. That's why I never put limits on myself."

—Keith Bulluck, on pushing himself to be better

"Pressure is what you make of it. It makes me play harder."

—Steve McNair, on playing your best in the clutch

"It was an exciting event, an exciting time. For us to play on a stage like that, it was definitely a dream come true. It felt like we belonged there."

—Eddie George, on making it to the Super Bowl

"Earl may not be in a class by himself, but whatever class he's in, it doesn't take long to call the roll."

—Bum Phillips on superstar Earl Campbell

"Everybody tells you how good you are, but you really don't know until you play against the best."

—George Webster, who starred for the Oilers from 1967 to 1972

"I don't think football is all that complicated."

—George Blanda, on keeping things simple as a quarterback

LEFT: Keith Bulluck
RIGHT: Bum Phillips

For the Record

T he great Oilers and Titans teams and players have left their marks on the record books. These are the "best of the best" ...

George Webster

Vince Young

TITANS AWARD WINNERS

WINNER	AWARD	YEAR
Lou Rymkus	AFL Coach of the Year	1960
George Blanda	AFL Most Valuable Player	1961
Wally Lemm	AFL Coach of the Year	1961
George Webster	AFL Rookie of the Year	1967
George Webster	AFL All-Star Game Defensive MVP	1969
Robert Brazile	Defensive Rookie of the Year	1975
Billy Johnson	Pro Bowl MVP	1976
Earl Campbell	Offensive Rookie of the Year	1978
Earl Campbell	Offensive Player of the Year	1978
Earl Campbell	Offensive Player of the Year	1979
Earl Campbell	NFL Most Valuable Player	1979
Earl Campbell	Offensive Player of the Year	1980
Warren Moon	Offensive Player of the Year	1990
Eddie George	Offensive Rookie of the Year	1996
Jevon Kearse	Defensive Rookie of the Year	1999
Steve McNair	NFL co-MVP	2003
Vince Young	Offensive Rookie of the Year	2006

TITANS ACHIEVEMENTS

ACHIEVEMENT	YEAR
AFL Eastern Division Champions	1960
AFL Champions	1960
AFL Eastern Division Champions	1961
AFL Champions	1961
AFL Eastern Division Champions	1962
AFL Eastern Division Champions	1967
AFC Central Champions	1991
AFC Central Champions	1993
AFC Champions	1999
AFC Central Champions	2000
AFC South Champions	2002

EDDIE **GEORGE**

TOP RIGHT: Eddie George
BOTTOM RIGHT: Warren Moon
BELOW: Earl Campbell

Pinpoints

The history of a football team is made up of many smaller stories. These stories take place all over the map—not just in the city a team calls "home." Match the pushpins on these maps to the Team Facts and you will begin to see the story of the Oilers and Titans unfold!

TEAM FACTS

1 Nashville, Tennessee—*The team has played here since 1998.*

2 Memphis, Tennessee—*The team played here as the Tennessee Oilers in 1997.*

3 Tiffin, Ohio—*Bill Groman was born here.*

4 Suffern, New York—*Keith Bulluck was born here.*

5 Philadelphia, Pennsylvania—*Eddie George was born here.*

6 Raleigh, North Carolina—*Bruce Matthews was born here.*

7 Fort Myers, Florida—*Jevon Kearse was born here.*

8 Bartlesville, Oklahoma—*Bud Adams was born here.*

9 Houston, Texas—*The team played here as the Oilers from 1960 to 1996.*

10 Tyler, Texas—*Earl Campbell was born here.*

11 Sonora, California—*Dan Pastorini was born here.*

12 Petronell, Austria—*Toni Fritsch was born here.*

Jevon Kearse

Play Ball

Football is a sport played by two teams on a field that is 100 yards long. The game is divided into four 15-minute quarters. Each team must have 11 players on the field at all times. The group that has the ball is called the offense. The group trying to keep the offense from moving the ball forward is called the defense.

A football game is made up of a series of "plays." Each play starts and ends with a referee's signal. A play begins when the center snaps the ball between his legs to the quarterback. The quarterback then gives the ball to a teammate, throws (or "passes") the ball to a teammate, or runs with the ball himself. The job of the defense is to tackle the player with the ball or stop the quarterback's pass. A play ends when the ball (or player holding the ball) is "down." The offense must move the ball forward at least 10 yards every four downs. If it fails to do so, the other team is given the ball. If the offense has not made 10 yards after three downs—and does not want to risk losing the ball—it can kick (or "punt") the ball to make the other team start from its own end of the field.

At each end of a football field is a goal line, which divides the field from the end zone. A team must run or pass the ball over the goal line to score a touchdown, which counts for six points. After scoring a touchdown, a team can try a short kick for one "extra point," or try again to run or pass across the goal line for two points. Teams can score three points from anywhere on the field by kicking the ball between the goal posts. This is called a field goal.

The defense can score two points if it tackles a player while he is in his own end zone. This is called a safety. The defense can also score points by taking the ball away from the offense and crossing the opposite goal line for a touchdown. The team with the most points after 60 minutes is the winner.

Football may seem like a very hard game to understand, but the more you play and watch football, the more "little things" you are likely to notice. The next time you are at a game, look for these plays:

PLAY LIST

BLITZ—A play where the defense sends extra tacklers after the quarterback. If the quarterback sees a blitz coming, he passes the ball quickly. If he does not, he can end up at the bottom of a very big pile!

DRAW—A play where the offense pretends it will pass the ball, and then gives it to a running back. If the offense can "draw" the defense to the quarterback and his receivers, the running back should have lots of room to run.

FLY PATTERN—A play where a team's fastest receiver is told to "fly" past the defensive backs for a long pass. Many long touchdowns are scored on this play.

SQUIB KICK—A play where the ball is kicked a short distance on purpose. A squib kick is used when the team kicking off does not want the other team's fastest player to catch the ball and run with it.

SWEEP—A play where the ball carrier follows a group of teammates moving sideways to "sweep" the defense out of the way. A good sweep gives the runner a chance to gain a lot of yards before he is tackled or forced out of bounds.

Glossary

FOOTBALL WORDS TO KNOW

AFC CHAMPIONSHIP—The game played to determine which AFC team will go to the Super Bowl.

AFL CHAMPIONSHIP—The game that decided the winner of the American Football League.

ALL-PRO—An honor given to the best players at their position at the end of each season.

AMERICAN FOOTBALL CONFERENCE (AFC)—One of two groups of teams that make up the National Football League. The winner of the AFC plays the winner of the National Football Conference (NFC) in the Super Bowl.

AMERICAN FOOTBALL LEAGUE (AFL)—The football league that began play in 1960 and later merged with the NFL.

BLOCK—Use the body to protect the ball carrier.

CANADIAN FOOTBALL LEAGUE—A professional league in Canada that began play in 1958.

DOUBLE-OVERTIME—The second extra period played when a game is tied after 60 minutes and a first extra period.

DRAFTED—Chosen from a group of the best college players. The NFL draft is held each spring.

DRIVE—A series of plays by the offense that "drives" the defense back toward its own goal line.

EASTERN DIVISION—A group of teams that play in the eastern part of the country.

FUMBLES—Balls that are dropped by the player carrying them.

HALL OF FAME—The museum in Canton, Ohio, where football's greatest players are honored. A player voted into the Hall of Fame is sometimes called a "Hall of Famer."

INTERCEPTIONS—Passes that are caught by the defensive team.

LATERAL—A pass backwards or sideways to a teammate.

MOST VALUABLE PLAYER (MVP)—The award given each year to the league's best player; also given to the best player in the Super Bowl and Pro Bowl.

NATIONAL FOOTBALL LEAGUE (NFL)—The league that started in 1920 and is still operating today.

NOSE TACKLE—The player in the middle of a three-man or five-man defensive line.

PLAYOFFS—The games played after the season to determine which teams play in the Super Bowl.

PRO BOWL—The NFL's all-star game, played after the Super Bowl.

PROFESSIONAL—A player or team that plays a sport for money.

ROOKIE OF THE YEAR—The annual award given to the league's best first-year player.

SACK—Tackle the quarterback behind the line of scrimmage.

SUPER BOWL—The championship of football, played between the winners of the NFC and AFC.

VETERANS—Players with great experience.

WILD CARD—A team that makes the playoffs without winning its division.

OTHER WORDS TO KNOW

CHARACTERS—Interesting or amusing people.

COLORFUL—Lively and interesting.

COMEBACK—The process of catching up from behind, or making up a large deficit.

DECADES—Periods of 10 years; also specific periods, such as the 1950s.

ERA—A period of time in history.

EXPERIENCED—Having knowledge and skill in a job.

FUNKY—Odd and entertaining.

LOGO—A symbol or design that represents a company or team.

MERGED—Joined forces.

MOUNTED—Moved or built into something bigger.

POTENTIAL—Possibility of becoming better.

PROMOTED—Given a better job.

STAMINA—The ability to sustain a long physical effort.

TAILBONE—The bone that protects the base of the spine.

TRADITION—A belief or custom that is handed down from generation to generation.

Places to Go

ON THE ROAD

TENNESSEE TITANS
One Titans Way
Nashville, Tennessee 37213
(615) 565-4000

THE PRO FOOTBALL HALL OF FAME
2121 George Halas Drive NW
Canton, Ohio 44708
(330) 456-8207

ON THE WEB

THE NATIONAL FOOTBALL LEAGUE   www.nfl.com
  • *Learn more about the National Football League*

THE TENNESSEE TITANS   www.titansonline.com
  • *Learn more about the Tennessee Titans*

THE PRO FOOTBALL HALL OF FAME   www.profootballhof.com
  • *Learn more about football's greatest players*

ON THE BOOKSHELF

To learn more about the sport of football, look for these books at your library or bookstore:

  • Fleder, Rob–Editor. *The Football Book*. New York, New York: Sports Illustrated Books, 2005.

  • Kennedy, Mike. *Football*. Danbury, Connecticut: Franklin Watts, 2003.

  • Savage, Jeff. *Play by Play Football*. Minneapolis, Minnesota: Lerner Sports, 2004.

Index

PAGE NUMBERS IN **BOLD** REFER TO ILLUSTRATIONS.

The Team

MARK STEWART has written more than 20 books on football, and over 100 sports books for kids. He grew up in New York City during the 1960s rooting for the Giants and Jets, and now takes his two daughters, Mariah and Rachel, to watch them play in their home state of New Jersey. Mark comes from a family of  writers. His grandfather was Sunday Editor of *The New York Times* and his mother was Articles Editor of *The Ladies' Home Journal* and *McCall's*. Mark has profiled hundreds of athletes over the last 20 years. He has also written several books about New York and New Jersey. Mark is a graduate of Duke University, with a degree in History. He lives with his daughters and wife Sarah overlooking Sandy Hook, New Jersey.

JASON AIKENS is the Collections Curator at the Pro Football Hall of Fame. He is responsible for the preservation of the Pro Football Hall of Fame's collection of artifacts and memorabilia and obtaining new donations of memorabilia from current players and NFL teams. Jason has a Bachelor of Arts in History from Michigan State University and a Master's in History from Western Michigan University where he concentrated on sports history. Jason  has been working for the Pro Football Hall of Fame since 1997; before that he was an intern at the College Football Hall of Fame. Jason's family has roots in California and has been following the St. Louis Rams since their days in Los Angeles, California. He lives with his wife Cynthia and their daughter Angelina in Canton, Ohio.